FULHAM
and
HAMMERSMITH

A Portrait in Old Picture Postcards

by

W. J. Drinkwater, P. J. Loobey and K. Whitehouse

S. B. Publications

First published in 1993 by S. B. Publications
c/o Grove Road, Seaford, East Sussex, BN25 1TP

ISBN 1 85770 046 5

Typeset, printed and bound by
Redwood Books, Trowbridge, Wiltshire

CONTENTS

THE AUTHORS

WILLIAM DRINKWATER lived and worked in the suburbs of Southall and Hornchurch for fifty years. After serving in the RAMC for the duration of World War II, he held positions with various London contractors and City firms before moving to Corsham, Wiltshire for his retirement.

Bill (an avid collector of old picture postcards and cigarette cards) has been widely published in magazine articles on an extensive range of subjects, including disablement, military matters, local history, short stories and collecting hobbies.

His book – *Southall/Norwood, A Portrait in Old Picture Postcards* – also published by S. B. Publications, was released in 1992 and takes a nostalgic look at the area in which he grew up. Sadly, Bill died in May, 1993 shortly after helping to complete the manuscript of this book and before its publication.

PATRICK LOOBEY, born in 1947, has lived in Balham, Putney, Southfields and Streatham – all within the London Borough of Wandsworth. He joined Wandsworth Historical Society in 1969 and has served on Archaeological, Publishing and Management Committees, being Chairman of the Society in 1991 and 1992. Having collected Edwardian postcards of Wandsworth Borough and the surrounding districts for 18 years, he has a wide-ranging collection encompassing many local roads and subjects.

Patrick has privately published a volume of postcard views on Putney and Rosehampton in 1988 and another on Battersea in 1990.

To obtain information regarding views published in this book, contact: Patrick J. Loobey, 231 Mitcham Lane, Streatham, London, SW16 6PY (Tel: 081–769–0072).

KEITH WHITEHOUSE was born in 1948 and lived in Fulham all his life. He established the Fulham Archaeological Rescue Group in 1972 and is currently director of rescue excavations. He is also a member of the Fulham and Hammersmith Historical Society and sits on the committees of the Fulham Society, the Friends of Fulham Palace and the Hammersmith and Fulham Historical Buildings Group. He is also president of the Hammersmith and District Philatelic Society.

INTRODUCTION

FULHAM AND HAMMERSMITH – a Portrait in Old Picture Postcards is not, as might seem at first sight, just a collection of nostalgic views of the district. Neither is it anything approaching an historical work – although each illustration is amply annotated with details which, it is hoped, will add a little to the reader's knowledge of the area. It does not either claim to be a guide book as such – but the photographs have been selected and placed in a certain sequence to enable those interested to carry out a perambulation from Putney Bridge to Shepherd's Bush. What then is it, that makes this book any different from the countless books published to a similar format throughout the country? Why is this collection so unusual – indeed, unique? The laymen can readily be forgiven for not knowing the answer, for only a specialist collector can be expected to know that. However, read on – all will become clear . . . !

It is essential then, to know a little of the outline history of the picture postcard to appreciate fully this publication. Plain postcards first appeared in Austria in 1869 and, the following year, in Britain. However, it was not until 1894 that postcards included a picture on the front. In 1902, the cards were standardised at $5\frac{1}{2}'' \times 3\frac{1}{2}''$ and messages allowed on the backs.

Between 1902 and 1914 there was a boom in the popularity of postcards. In 1906, an estimated 264 million were sent in this country and the craze for collecting and storing in albums became a popular pastime until 1918 when the postal rate doubled from $\frac{1}{2}$d. to 1d. The picture postcard remained the cheapest means of communication for over 20 years – a period now referred to as 'The Golden Age of Postcards'.

Postcards were produced in several different ways. Small local firms reproduced photographic cards from an original in small batches. The quality of the copy was determined by the skill of the photographer in the developing process. The caption on the front was often a handwritten addition. Some larger firms were set up of publishers using local photographers using a mass production technique of contact printing from a negative onto a machine, thus producing great quantities. National postcard publishers like Frith, Judge's and Valentine's sprang up – many based in London. Little wonder is it, therefore, that with two world wars and the subsequent bombing of the Capital, that few postcard publishers of the old days still exist. Their work today can be found in dealers' boxes at postcard fairs, in the hands of ardent collectors and elderly members of the public who still treasure them.

Patrick Loobey can rightly claim himself to be one of today's most discerning collectors of old picture postcards – specialising in many of the Boroughs skirting the Thames. Over the years he has scoured the country, frequenting the regular postcard fairs in search of his particular postcard memorabilia and, as Pat's collection increased, one name – JOHNS – became dominant on the cards.

A search through Kelly's and the Post Office Directories of 1912–13 revealed the first entries for a postcard publisher R. J. Johns & Co., as carrying on business at 171 Longley Road, Tooting. In 1920, the firm was listed as R. J. Johns, photographic publishers – then in 1921, as Maycock and Johns, photographic publishers. In 1924 they seem to have parted company, for the name Maycock appears alone and Johns and Sons, photographers, appears at 144 Northcote Road, Battersea, approximately $1\frac{1}{2}$ miles from Longley Road. Little more is known as to what became of Johns and his business, but, in 1987, came an incredible happening . . .

A lady, clearing out the attic of her house in Mitcham, Surrey, discovered an amazingly large collection of glass-plate negatives of lively street scenes taken around the London areas of the City and West End, Banstead, Dulwich, Hampton, Kennington, Peckham, Putney, Tooting, Golders Green, Hampstead, Wimbledon and Wokingham. Although immediately snapped up by London Boroughs in the main, Pat was in time to buy up some 2,500 of the negatives covering Fulham, Chelsea, Hammersmith, Acton, Shepherd's Bush, Chiswick, Golders Green and others.

It is therefore, from this find and Pat's own card collection, that this book comes. What makes it so unique is that, from cover to cover, it is filled with Johns' pictures. They give us a glimpse of what Fulham and Hammersmith looked like from 1912 onwards. Thus, the reader will be able to compare with today and note the changes – and there have been many.

Gone are a number of theatres and cinemas – The Granville Theatre of Varieties, The Grand Theatre, The King's Theatre, the Hammersmith Palace of Varieties, The Blue Halls and The Star Kinema. Places of worship have disappeared as well as those of amusement, for example, the Munster Park Methodist Chapel, the West End Baptist Chapel and the classical building of the Oaklands Congregational Church. The magnificent Old Town Hall, Hammersmith has been demolished, as has St. Paul's School for Boys, which numbered amongst its 'old boys' General Montgomery. The reader is also urged to spare a glance – while still possible – at the Shepherd's Bush Empire, its future being somewhat uncertain.

However, the greater the change, the greater the interest in things of yesteryear . . . in what things used to be like in the world that has passed in the mist of time. Nothing brings back memories of the days of yore and reveals the transformations that Fulham and Hammersmith have undergone, as well as old photographs. It is hoped that this collection will appease the appetites of older residents, satisfy the curiosity of new ones (especially those from foreign lands) and encourage further research by others.

None of those who know the area today, or knew it in days past, cannot, one feels, but be fascinated by the array of nostalgia presented between the covers of this book.

W. J. Drinkwater

Putney Bridge, c. 1912

Built as a replacement to Fulham Bridge (1729) in 1886. Designed by Sir Joseph Bazelgette. This view shows the bridge's original width before it was widened in 1933.

All Saints' Church, Fulham, c. 1912

The ancient parish church is first recorded in 1154 but has probably stood on this site for well over 1,000 years. The tower is the oldest standing building in Hammersmith and Fulham, under construction by 1440. The body of the church was completely rebuilt in 1881 by the architect Sir Arthur Blomfield (1829–99) who was born at Fulham Palace, his father being the Bishop of London. Pryor's Bank is on the left, named after a Gothic house built in 1837 and demolished in 1897. The site is now occupied by the offices of the Parks Department.

The Iron Bridge, Putney, c. 1912

The 'Iron Bridge' (it has no other name) was built in 1889 when the Metropolitan District Railway was extended from Fulham to Wimbledon. The bridge is actually owned by British Rail, not London Underground. To the left is Putney Bridge Station which, when built in 1880, was called Putney Bridge and Fulham Station. In 1902 it became Putney Bridge and Hurlingham Station when the Hurlingham Club was highly fashionable, but in 1932 the present name was given. Fulham had its own river pier by the bridge before the First World War.

The Grand Theatre, Putney Bridge Approach, c. 1922

The Grand Theatre was built in 1897 and Ellen Terry, Julia Neilson and Sarah Bernhardt were among the stars who appeared there. It closed in the 1930s and was demolished in the late 1950s to make way for the ICL office building. On the left is the King's Arms public house, an old coaching inn first recorded as existing in the early 16th century but rebuilt in 1888.

Fulham House, Fulham High Street, c. 1912

Fulham House was built about 1740 and, since 1902, has been a Territorial Army Centre. During the 1980s it was threatened with demolition but has now been renovated. During the renovation 18th-century wallpaper was found still on the walls; this has been expertly removed and preserved.

The 25th (City of London) Cyclist Battalion, c. 1912

The 25th (C of L) Cyclist Battalion was based at Fulham House. This view was taken in Bishop's Avenue. The boy on the right appears completely unimpressed by the occasion.

Fulham High Street, c. 1912

Fulham High Street was the principal road of Fulham Manor and first appears in records in 1391 when it was known as 'Burystrete', a Saxon word referring to it lying within the defensive earthworks of Fulham Palace. In the picture can be seen a no. 44 bus on route to Putney Common.

The King's Head, Fulham High Street, c. 1915

The King's Head dates from 1906, but the earliest record of a public house on this site dates from 1695. This was replaced in 1884 by a new pub which only survived until 1906 when the whole of the west side of the High Street was demolished for widening when trams came to this part of Fulham.

Fulham Palace Road, Facing North, c. 1914

This was formerly the northern end of Fulham High Street which ended at Bishop's Avenue. On the left is Bishop's Park and on the right the houses are built on an outer earthwork of the Palace defences, formerly known as High Bank. These houses are now showing signs of subsidence. The trams came through here until 1935 when they were replaced by trolley buses.

Fulham Palace, c. 1912

The Manor of Fulham was purchased by the Bishop of London in A.D. 704 and Fulham Palace was a popular country estate. In the 18th century it became their official residence until 1973 when the Church Commissioners leased the Palace and gardens to the Borough Council. Plans included a museum, art gallery and public use, but most of the rooms have remained empty or under-used. This view shows the Western Quadrangle built during the 15th/16th century. On the left is the Great Hall, built about 1480. The fountain, designed by Butterfield, dated from the 1880s.

The Chapel, Fulham Palace, c. 1912

Known as the Tait Chapel after Bishop Tait (1856–68) who commissioned the building, designed by the eminent architect, William Butterfield, and dedicated to the Blessed Trinity, 1st May, 1867. To the left is the Cork Oak planted by Bishop Henry Compton (1675–1713), one of the many rare trees and plants introduced by him from America. It unfortunately no longer survives.

Fulham Palace, Bishop Howley's Dining Room, c. 1924

This room was built by the architect Samuel Pepys Cockerell circa 1814. It has recently been renovated and occupied by the Museum of Fulham Palace exhibiting displays on the Palace's history.

The Avenue and Moat, Bishop's Park, c. 1912

The moat of Fulham Palace is one of the enigmas of Fulham's history. It was first mentioned in documents in 1392, although tradition has associated it with a Danish Viking army which camped in the area in A.D. 880–881. Archaeological excavations have suggested it is much older, possibly dating back to pre-Roman times, being a defensive enclosure around a settlement. Neolithic occupation (circa 3000 B.C.) and a Roman settlement have been discovered here. Some of the finds may be seen in the Museum of Fulham Palace. The moat was once filled with fresh water and well stocked with fish, but, due to its insanitary state, it was filled in from 1921.

The Sands, Bishop's Park, Fulham, c. 1912

The Sands, or Margate Sands (said to be where the sand came from) was opened in 1903 and was very popular with children. The houses of Stevenage Road may be seen in the background. Bishop's Park was opened in 1893.

Fulham Road, c. 1912

Fulham Road is one of the oldest roads in the area and may date back to prehistoric times, connecting with a ford which crossed the Thames near Putney Bridge. On the right is a London, Midland & Scottish parcels van. In the background can be seen Drive Mansions.

Burnfoot Avenue, Fulham, c. 1912
A typical late Victorian Street. The attention is immediately caught by the absence of cars.

Fulham Road, Junction with Munster Road, c. 1912

Looking towards the Munster Park Methodist Chapel which has now been demolished. On the left stood Munster House. 'Munster' comes from 'Mustow', a district of Fulham first recorded in the 14th century. The name may mean 'the meeting place of the moot', or people's council in Saxon times.

Fulham Fire Station, Fulham Road, c. 1912

Fulham Fire Station was built in 1896 by the L.C.C. adjacent to the earlier fire station which dated from about 1869. With only two appliances at first, a third was added later with fire escape ladders. Notice the watch tower – a necessary, view-point from where to pinpoint fires before most people had telephones. At present, the building is being refurbished at a cost of several million pounds and the facade is to be cleaned, greatly improving this listed landmark.

New Kings Road, Fulham, c. 1912

New Kings Road was originally the King's Private road, although the road has existed for centuries. Charles I made it a private road so that it could be kept in good repair, being the route between St. James's Palace and Hampton Court. There were six gates along its route, looked after by gate-keepers and a metal token was issued to those who were authorised to use it. Due to increased traffic and public pressure, it was thrown open as a public road in 1830.

Coniger Road, Fulham, c. 1912

One of the typical streets of the Peterborough Estate commenced in 1888, built over the grounds of Peterborough House, a fine classical mansion constructed in 1798 near the site of an earlier Peterborough House but demolished about 1901. Notice the lions on the roof, a common feature on this estate built by local builder, Jimmy Nichols.

Parson's Green, c. 1925

Adjoining these houses is St. Dionis' Church, built in 1885 on the site of the ancient rectory. Next to it is the church hall, formerly the Parson's Green Mission Hall, erected in 1876, where services were held before the church was built. The benefactor was Miss Charlotte Sulivan of Broom House.

Lady Margaret School, Parson's Green, c. 1925

Two young ladies probably on their way to or from school. Lady Margaret School was established in 1917 and consists of three old houses. This view shows Belfield House which dates back to at least the early 18th century and was, at one time, occupied by Mrs. Jordan, the mistress of the Duke of Clarence, later William IV. The school is still flourishing.

Parson's Green, c. 1922

Two men sit and watch the world go by at Parsons Green which takes the name from the rectory or parsonage that stood on the site of St. Dionis' Church. The name first appears in documents in the 14th century. On the left in this view is the Duke of Cumberland public house on the corner of Peterborough Road, formerly the Duke's Head which has stood here since 1861.

Eelbrook Common, adjoining New Kings Road, c. 1912

Eelbrook Common is first mentioned in 1410 as 'Hillebrook' – 'The stream by the hill'. The stream formed a pond where St. John's Church, Walham Green, now stands and flowed through the Broadway across the Common and down Bagley's Lane into the Thames. The hill survives as Musgrave Crescent. In the 1880s the Metropolitan Board of Works bought the Common from the freeholders, the Church Commissioners.

Wandsworth Bridge Road, c. 1912

Wandsworth Bridge Road was built as a new road connecting Wandsworth Bridge with the New Kings Road, built in 1873.
The scene with the children standing in the middle of the road would be almost impossible to reproduce today.

Sandilands Road, c. 1912

Small cottage-type houses in Sandilands Road with one of the gas-holders of Fulham Gasworks visible in the distance. The road was named after the Rev. Sandilands. Note the complete absence of any type of vehicle.

Wandsworth Bridge Road, c. 1925
A bustling scene in 1925 – and today it still has a busy shopping area.

Star Kinema, Wandsworth Bridge Road, c. 1912

This popular cinema, which stood at the corner of Broughton Road Approach, is now demolished.

Hazelbury Road, c. 1922

The customary scene of children in the street. Hazelbury Road was one of a series of similar streets forming the Hever Estate built from the 1880s. Others are Cranbury, Rosebury and Snowbury.

Broomhouse Lane, Showing Schools, c. 1912

Broomhouse was a hamlet first recorded in the 15th century. It takes its name from broom, the yellow flowering bush which grows on sandy soils whose twigs were also used to sweep the floor. On the left are the grounds of Broom House and, on the right, Wilson's Cottage, while the Elizabethan Schools can be seen in the distance.

The Schools, Broomhouse Road, c. 1912

The Elizabethan Schools, built in 1855 as a ragged charity school (for children too dirty for any other school) with two almshouses attached, by the Hon. Laurence Sulivan of Broom House, which stood on the other side of Broomhouse Lane. Constructed in memory of his wife, Elizabeth, sister of Lord Palmerston, the famous Prime Minister – hence the Elizabethan style. Broom House was bought by the Hurlingham Club in 1912 and demolished, but its gardens are now part of the Club grounds. The 'school' is now used by the Borough Council's Education Department and is on a preservation list.

Wilson's Cottage, Broomhouse Road, c. 1912

One of the quaint pantiled cottages that were still to be seen in Fulham early this century.

Carnwath Cottage, Fulham, c. 1914
A typical weatherboarded, pantiled cottage. In the distance is Hugon Road School.

Peterborough Road, Fulham, c. 1914

Formerly an old lane first mentioned in the 17th century, connecting Parson's Green with the riverside area. Notice the hand-pushed dairy cart on the left.

Peterborough School, c. 1914

Peterborough School, as viewed from the South Park, was built in 1901 by the London School Board. It is typical of the superb school buildings constructed at this time.

Hurlingham House, c. 1914

Hurlingham House (Listed Grade II*) as we see it today, was built about 1800, but the central part dates to 1760, when it was erected for Dr. Cadogan, an eminent physician. Famous residents include the Marquis Wellesley, the Duke of Wellington's brother, and several Governors of the Bank of England. In 1869 it became the Hurlingham Club (a pigeon shooting club) and grew into a very fashionable establishment still thriving today.

Polo at Hurlingham, c. 1914

Polo at Hurlingham was introduced in 1874 – just five years after being brought to England – and became the headquarters of British polo. The two polo fields were compulsorily purchased after the War by the London County Council. No. 2 is covered by the Sulivan Court Council Housing Estate. No. 1 is now Hurlingham Park. The Polo grandstand now used for athletic events was built in 1935 – it is now little-used and, being in need of much repair, the Borough Council is planning to demolish it.

Fulham Town Hall, c. 1912

Fulham Town Hall was built in 1890 with later extensions. This view was taken from Harwood Road, named after a local landowner.

Fulham Broadway, c. 1912

A busy picture showing Fulham Broadway which became the centre of Fulham from 1890 when the town hall was built here.

Fulham Broadway Station, c. 1912

Fulham Broadway Station was called Walham Green until 1952. Local traders thought the name was too rural and wanted to emulate Hammersmith Broadway. Built in 1880 when the Metropolitan District Railway came here, the attractive station facade was added in the early 20th century.

The Broadway, Walham Green, c. 1912

Walham Green was one of the villages of Fulham first mentioned in 1383. It had a pond (now the site of St. John's Church) and a village green (centre) occupied in this view by a fine bank built in the Queen Anne style in the 1890s, unfortunately demolished in the 1970s. The architecturally dull Fulham Centre now stands on the site.

The Granville Theatre of Varieties, Walham Green, c. 1914

The Granville Theatre was built by Dan Leno, the famous music hall star. Designed by the theatre architect, Frank Matcham (creator of The London Coliseum and old Lyric Theatre) it opened in 1898 and among the stars who have appeared there have been Marie Lloyd, George Robey and Little Titch. Of note was its beautiful interior of glazed and majolica tilework. After World War II, it became a film studio but was destroyed in 1971 after an unsuccessful campaign to save it. Due to the way the demolition had been granted by the Borough Council, the Greater London Council's Historic Buildings Division listed other important theatres in London.

The Red Hall, Vanston Place, Fulham, c. 1912

Built just before World War I as a cinema, The Red Hall later became The Walham Green Gaumont. It is now a Bingo Hall with the facade much altered and the bronze statue of Mercury removed.

The Butchers' Almshouses, Vanston Place, Fulham, c. 1912

The Butchers' Charitable Institution Almshouses (to give their full title) were erected in 1840 for the benefit of those employed in the meat and hide trades, their widows and orphans. They were demolished in 1922 to make way for the Samuel Lewis Trust Dwellings.

Walham Green, North End Road, c. 1912

North End Road was originally a country lane that connected with the village of North End either side of the road. On the right is the Church of St. John, built on the site of the village pond infilled in 1814.

North End Road, Corner of Sedlescombe Road, c. 1912

First mentioned in the 15th century, North End Road was the road from Walham Green to Hammersmith Road. The hamlet of North End lay either side. It is now famous for its street market, mainly selling fruit and vegetables, which it has done for over 100 years.

Lillie Road, c. 1925

On the left of this view is the Half Way Public House built on the front garden of an earlier 19th century house. Lillie Road (formerly Crown Lane) was named after Major-General Sir John Scott Lillie who constructed the eastern section between North End Road and Lillie Bridge in the 1820s.

Fulham Cross, Junction of Lillie and Munster Roads, c. 1925
The name appears to date only from the 19th century, i.e. 'where the roads cross'.

Bishop's Road, c. 1925

Bishop's Road was so named in 1879. In origin, a very old lane extending from Dawes Road to Colehill Lane connecting Walham Green with Fulham High Street.

Mirabel Road, Fulham, c. 1912

Mirabel Road was built in 1886. This picture is taken looking towards Dawes Road. Note the cast iron railings, removed during the Second World War to assist the war effort.

St. Thomas of Canterbury Church, Rylston Road, c. 1914

The Church of St. Thomas of Canterbury was constructed in 1847 to the designs of Augustus Welby Pugin. This Roman Catholic Church was a gift of Mrs. Elizabeth Bowden. Built in the open fields, it became a notable landmark. The churchyard holds the remains of the architect, Herbert Gribble (1894), designer of the Brompton Oratory; A. W. Taylor (1879), William Morris' business manager (the tombstone being designed by Philip Webb) and Joseph Hansom (1882) architect and inventor of the hansom cab.

Fulham Palace Road, c. 1920

Ellaline Road can be seen on the left of this scene. Notice the no. 11 open-top bus. These 'B' type buses were in use between 1910 and 1926 and many were used in World War I to take troops to the trenches in France.

Larnarch Road, c. 1925

One of a series of similar roads built as the Crabtree Estate from 1911 on the site of Crabtree Farm. In 1910, Edward Matyear, whose family had farmed the area since the 18th century, died without issue and left the farm to the King Edward VII Hospital Fund, who sold the land by auction to Allen & Norris. Sir Henry Norris was Mayor of Fulham and subsequently Conservative M.P. A selling feature of these houses was that they had electricity and a purpose-built bathroom. The scene shows three boys with a pedal push-car in the roadway.

Riverside Children's Outing, 1926

This outing of 1926 is typical of its period. Dorset Wharf, Rainville Road, takes its name from Dorset Villa which stood on this site until 1890.

Fulham Palace Road looking towards St. Dunstan's Road, c. 1914

Biscay Road is on the left. Notice the advertisements with names that are still with us – *The News of the World*, R. White's Lemonade and the Earls Court Exhibition Centre.

The Infirmary, Fulham Palace Road, c. 1912

This is now the site of Charing Cross Hospital, formerly Fulham Hospital which grew out of the Fulham Workhouse or Union, established here in 1849. This part of Fulham Palace Road was, in the later 19th century, known as Union Road.

Fulham Palace Road, c. 1914

The Rifle public house, on the corner of Distillery Lane, is now called the Golden Gloves. The next corner is Chancellor's Road, the boundary between Fulham and Hammersmith. Notice the three golden balls (the sign of the pawnbroker) and the Distillers Arms public house, still thriving.

Hammersmith Bridge, c. 1914

Hammersmith Bridge was built in 1887 for the Metropolitan Board of Works and designed by their engineer, Sir Joseph Bazelgette, on the stone piers of an earlier suspension bridge constructed in 1827. Although much loved today, William Morris in *News From Nowhere* refers to it as an 'ugly suspension bridge'.

Lower Mall, Hammersmith, c. 1914
The building marked with an 'X' is Kent House, built about 1750.

Lower Mall, Hammersmith, c. 1914

The Rutland Hotel, a public house, is still there, although it lost its top floor during World War II. The West End Boat House on the left is now gone, being replaced by private flats. In the background is Hammersmith Bridge.

Queen Caroline Street, Hammersmith, c. 1915

The bus garage was built in 1913 on the site of Bradmore House. The garden frontage was carefully taken down and rebuilt as the front of the garage, allowance being made for two large doors to let the buses in and out. At present, the site is being redeveloped and the facade restored, windows reinstated, with a new building behind to be used as a restaurant and offices.

Hammersmith Broadway, c. 1915

A policeman keeps an eye open for any problems (or is he admiring the large motor-car?). The view shows the old Town Hall in Shepherd's Bush Road. This magnificent building was, regrettably demolished in the 1960s.

Hammersmith Station, Hammersmith Broadway, c. 1914

This attractive facade proudly displaying G(reat) N(orthern) Piccadilly & Brompton Railway, opened in 1906, has recently been demolished as part of the island site redevelopment by Bredero and London Transport.

St. Paul's School, Hammersmith Road, c. 1922

St. Paul's School for Boys was founded by Dean Colet in 1509 and moved to Hammersmith in 1884 to a newly-built school designed by the eminent architect William Waterhouse. In 1969 the school moved to Barnes and this outstanding Gothic building in red brick and terracotta was, despite its Grade II listing and enormous public protest demolished by the I.L.E.A. The school and its playing fields is now covered by the West London College and housing. During World War II, the 21 Army Group under Gen. Montgomery, a former pupil, was based here and planned the invasion of Europe.

The Kings Theatre, Hammersmith, c. 1915

Built in 1902, The Kings Theatre stood in the
Hammersmith Road on the corner of Rowan Road.
According to the poster, 'The Glad Eye' was the
play being (or about to be) performed at the time
the picture was taken. This very popular theatre
closed in 1954 and was demolished in 1963 to make
way for an anonymous office building.

Hammersmith Broadway, 1915

The man in the centre of the view finds time to lean on a bollard (not a lamp-post as in the song by George Formby!). Has he just emerged from the Swan public house on the left? This rather imposing building was built in 1901. Behind is the Great Western & Metropolitan Line Station in Beadon Road opened 1864.

Hammersmith Broadway, c. 1924
A busy scene showing Palmer's Store at the corner of King Street and Queen Caroline Street.

Blacks Road, Hammersmith, c. 1924

This view shows the rear of Palmer's Store and the Hop Poles public house on the extreme left. Notice the open-top bus.

King Street, Hammersmith, c. 1914

This scene shows it was as busy then as it is now. Note the commissionaire in his uniform proudly standing outside the Cinematograph Theatre.

King Street, Hammersmith, c. 1914

Palmer's Store, King Street, opened in 1886. This was a very popular department store. It closed in the 1950s and the building was demolished in the 1980s.

King Street, Hammersmith, near Weltje Road, c.1912

Are the two boys debating whether they can afford an ice? Sadly, the buildings on the right were removed during the 1930s to widen King Street.

King Street, Hammersmith, c. 1915
King Street is part of the Great West Road – the Roman route from London to Bath and on to Bristol. It is now superseded by the A4 constructed in the 1950s.

The Blue Halls, King Street, c. 1915

The Blue Halls were two cinemas in one building built in 1913. They were demolished when the Hammersmith Town Hall was constructed in the 1930s.

Hammersmith Palace of Varieties, King Street, c. 1914

An example of a music hall growing out of a public house; the Town Hall Tavern in the 1880s, closed in 1940 and the building was demolished in 1950.

King Street, Facing East, c. 1915

The Electric Palace Cinema can be seen on the right in this picture and the Plough & Harrow public house on the left. This was turned into a motorcar showroom in the 1950s and is now selling Rolls Royce cars (rather an achievement for a building – pub to elegant car showroom!). In the distance can be seen the tower of the Palace of Varieties.

75

Dalling Road, Hammersmith, c. 1914

Formerly Webbs Lane. Near here stood a Leper Hospital which was in existence by the year 1500.

The West End Chapel, King Street, Hammersmith, c. 1914

Built by the local Baptists in 1851, this dignified building was demolished in the 1960s to make way for the overbearing architecture of the Polish Centre.

Latymer School for Boys, King Street, Hammersmith, c. 1914

This is the oldest school in Hammersmith, being set up with money left by Edward Latymer, who owned property locally, in 1627 to educate eight poor Hammersmith boys. The present school buildings were erected from 1895.

Ravenscourt House, c. 1914

Swans enjoy a peaceful moment on the lake under the willow-tree. Ravenscourt House was a public library until it was destroyed by an air-raid in 1941. Formerly known as Palingswick, the name can be traced back to the 13th century. During the 14th century it was owned by Alice Perrers, mistress of Edward III. The Corbett family bought the house and, in the 1750s, changed the name to Ravenscourt (Corbeau is French for raven). The Scott family sold the house and grounds to the Metropolitan Board of Works (later the London County Council) who turned the gardens into a public park in 1888.

Ravenscourt Square, c. 1914
Ravenscourt Square adjoins Ravenscourt Park. This Italianate house still stands.

St. Peter's Square, c. 1914

A speculative development on the edge of Hammersmith built in the 1820s, St. Peter's Square is now one of the most fashionable parts of Hammersmith. The architect is unknown, bu the central garden was laid out by the celebrated landscape gardener, J. C. Loudon.

St. Peter's Church, St. Peter's Square, Hammersmith, c. 1914

Built in 1829, in the then fashionable Greco-Roman style, to serve the new development. Designed by the architect Edward Lapidge who, at one time, lived in Fulham High Street.

The Synagogue, Brook Green, c. 1914

Brook Green dates back to medieval times and takes its name from a tributary of the Stamford Brook that flowed across the Green and became the boundary between Hammersmith and Fulham.

Uxbridge Road Station, Shepherd's Bush, c. 1914

Uxbridge Road Station, built by the West London Railway, was opened in 1869 and closed in 1940. It stood to the east of the main entrance to the exhibition in Uxbridge Road (see photo no. 85). Lockharts dining room was an eating-house popular after cinema or theatre performances.

Shepherd's Bush Tube Station, c. 1914

Adjoining the main entrance to the White City Exhibition Centre. Originally built in 1908 for the Franco-British Exhibition, this large area (well over 100 acres) also housed a stadium used to stage the Olympic Games in that year. Major exhibitions took place here annually until the outbreak of World War I. Most of the buildings are now demolished and the site is largely covered by the White City Council Housing Estate and the BBC Television Centre. The last major building to go was the Stadium, used until recent years for greyhound racing. The entrance in this view still survives, but devoid of its decoration and turrets.

Uxbridge Road, c. 1924

Shepherd's Bush Green on the right. The clock on the corner says half-past-three, just the time for a visit to Lyons Tea-Room on the right of the picture (a common site at one time).

Shepherd's Bush Green, South Side, c. 1914

Shepherd's Bush first appears in documents in the 17th century and was not of any consequence. The area was developed in the 19th century, the railway coming here as early as the 1840s.

Shepherd's Bush Empire, c. 1914

Until recently the BBC Television Theatre, it was built as the Shepherd's Bush Empire Music Hall in 1903 by Sir Oswald Stoll. Stars appearing her included Harry Lauder, Dan Leno, Marie Lloyd, George Robey and Vesta Tilley. The future of this imposing listed building is uncertain.

The Green, Shepherd's Bush, c. 1924
This view has been taken facing north. An interesting variety of ways to get about – on foot, bicycle, motor car or bus.

Wood Lane, Shepherd's Bush, c. 1914

This imposing structure is the entrance to the White City Exhibition. The Anglo-American Exposition was open in 1914, but closed after a few months due to the outbreak of World War I. This was the last major public exhibition to be held here. The exhibitions were organised by a Hungarian, Imre Kiralfy. Although the buildings were covered in white stucco, the name White City came from the Chicago Columbian Exhibition which Kiralfy visited in 1893.

Shepherd's Bush Library, c. 1914

Situated in Goldhawk Road, corner of Pennard Road, this handsome building in red brick and stone was built in 1899 and
is typical of the type of public building being erected at this time. 'Civic Pride' was then at the forefront.

Lime Grove, Shepherd's Bush, c. 1914
This quiet Victorian Street is now well-known for its associations with early British films and the BBC, being the site of the
former Lime Grove Film Studios opened around 1910.

Oaklands Congregational Church, c. 1914

Built in 1857, Oaklands Congregational Church was situated on the corner of Uxbridge Road and Oaklands Grove on land given by Peter Broad. This attractive classical building has only been demolished in recent years.

Goldhawk Road, c. 1914

Goldhawk Road appears to have originated as a Roman road that had fallen into disuse by medieval times and was re-opened in the early 19th century as the New Road. Goldhawk were a family who lived in the area in the 15th century. In the middle 19th century it was lined with handsome villas.

The Pond, Goldhawk Road, c. 1919

A gardener pauses from his watering to gaze at this peaceful scene. The pond was situated at Starch Green, Hammersmith, junction of Goldhawk Road and Askew Road. It was infilled from 1926 and is now an open space. Another name for this area was Gagglegoose Green.

Goldhawk Road, c. 1914

Goldhawk Road with the Half Moon and Seven Stars public house standing on the corner of Paddenswick Road is still there, although the cinema next door has now gone.